"ALL ARE BORN AS ORIGINALS, BUT MANY DIE AS PHOTOCOPIES."

BLESSED CARLO ACUTIS

Made in the USA
Monee, IL
06 June 2024

59422730R00057